I0756237

FINISHING LINE PRESS
www.finishinglinepress.com

Lotus Earth on Fire

poems by

Lynn Axelrod

Finishing Line Press
Georgetown, Kentucky

Lotus Earth on Fire

Rainer Maria Rilke's Gravity's Law:
How surely gravity's law,/strong as an ocean current,/takes hold of the smallest thing/and pulls it toward the heart of the world. [...] Each thing—/ each stone, blossom, child—/is held in place.

Rainer Maria Rilke, *The Book of Hours*, II:16

ISBN 979-8-88838-563-0 First Edition

ACKNOWLEDGMENTS

Grateful acknowledgment to the following literary journals and outlets where some of these poems first appeared, some in a slightly different version:

Birdland Journal, How May We Be, birdlandjournal.com
California Quarterly, I Zoomed Into The Reading
Marin Poetry Center Anthology, Our Year In Four
Medical Literary Messenger, After The Diagnosis
Pandemic Puzzle Poems anthology, Breathing Room, Blue Light Press, 2022
Pendemic.ie (Irish Poetry Reading Archive, Univ. College Dublin), How Much
Poetry Lovers' Daily Poem, They Say Fire Is A Metaphor, lists.sonic.net/mailman/listinfo/poetrylovers
Poetry X Hunger, Gleaning, poetryxhunger.com
San Francisco Chronicle, Vanessa Hua column, You're Invited, vanessahua.com, "[selected] Poems of Gratitude by Bay Area Readers"
The Avocet, Bird Watching
The Weekly Avocet, Between Tides; Generations; Incarnata

Publisher: Leah Huete de Maines
Editor: Christen Kincaid
Cover Art: Dave Mitchell, sparselysageandtimely.com
Author Photo: Dave Mitchell, sparselysageandtimely.com
Cover Design: Elizabeth Maines McCleavy

Order online: www.finishinglinepress.com
also available on amazon.com

Author inquiries and mail orders:
Finishing Line Press
PO Box 1626
Georgetown, Kentucky 40324
USA

Contents

Our Year In Four

[Winter]

Bird-call makes us break our solitude and sleep
to slip within this risen day.
The water bowl's resurgent lake, clear enough
for sparrow-sip this warming day.
Bird-track stars in snow crystals
deliver us this glistening day.
Prints recede as skimming seeds
hail this breath of day.

[Spring]

Emerge from where we go, hopeless captives
who fail to hobble dreams that make us quake
at what we keep from what we may release
like birdsong calling in the day.
Gaping redwings, shoulders back, slingshot notes
around the meadow,
our neighborly divide their forum.
Swainsons' swirling flutes swizzle 'cross the treetops.
We cast our husks of tribute—sunflower, millet, suet—
to charm the scrubland gods: While time is light
as breath is air, send them here
these newborn days.

[Summer]

Indigo sky.
No shoes, no shirt.
No rules need apply.
Berries lie in beds we made, testifying to our pride,
our lustful spring ambition.
Luscious unclaimed virgins no one ate or tried
    jumped—or were they pushed—
from overcrowded vines, juices caking in the dust.
Laboring emmets carry off the spoils,
clamber up the stalks;
roving antennae fondle aphid rears:
honeydew!—like cheap, sweet beer.
Crusading leagues of ladybugs

arrive to save the plants from habituated ants
who fight to keep their hooch.
Skirmish on the ragged green,
lunges, bites, maneuvers.
Biology is destiny, we say—
irrelevant to the sun devouring the day.

[Fall]

Bring the tools inside, lay them sharp,
always clean, at rest in the dark.
The turned earth settles cool above,
warming continents below.
Give us time to think goodbye
sit on cushioned chairs
puzzle birds their silent pluming flights
wonder how they are.
Which tilt was final; setting sun decisive?
We try to reason when they knew: 'now' not if.
Storing wood for the annual surrender
we stake the ground on tremors
unbuckling chasms, bargaining again
we'll hear the faintest notes return
sometimes through a murmur—raucous, rising.
Earth heaves, shudders in its own oscillation.

How Much

Low stream flows, deceptively gentle
incubate fish eggs, keep them safe,
while storms would sweep them away
toward predators downstream.

Birthing salmon and steelhead, fins flinch,
shudder in waters too calm for swimming
to tributaries, their birth canals.

In the main stem, they dig up
each other's eggs, lay their own. Animals
fond of *ikura*, meaning 'salmon eggs'
and also 'how much,' quickly feast.

Sword of storm, sword of calm hangs above.
How often we celebrate, scoop caviar,
lives swallowed like casual swords
cutting through first life.

Custom of delicate spoons, as if fearing
fragility of wealth, prone to slip away,
glistening pearly ounces, as if
taking less dignifies the taking, as if

life's thrashings disappear beneath
gleaming dishes of roe, as if
too much would reveal our gaze
deciding who survives cycles,
dying, reviving.

Fish ache to fly upstream like birds
swim through clouds like blooms
welcome the sun, as fawns bond
in faint cries to their does.
Doe and fawn graze, lie on grass,
each blade holding its own weight.

They Say Fire Is A Metaphor

We weren't ready for everything to go.
We told some gods
we were grateful for what we had
—a paltry thing against infernos.

We search for lost ones through what remains
—cement angels, crazed rock, melted
metal cast as pyres—incinerated
by refusal electeds dare not explain.

Broken voices reached us on ether,
discovered their own breath
still ninety-eight point six but choked
like a ghost with fever.

Ash lungs—tea of celestial spider webs,
throats clogged—no relief. Yellow sky.
Clouds swirled like ply unraveling,
smoldering threads.

Brigades of birds shot out, circling alone,
nestlings agape, flame-fed
calls crossed woven twigs, grass,
ephemera destined for indeterminate bone.

Blanketed babes wound in arms for cradles,
ash where they stopped, unsifted mix
of wool, milk, grain, bleached of sound.
Only wind trembles.

Twisted trees, charred limbs affright.
Rivers of dust will follow,
swallow trunks, leave glistening stone
arbors twice petrified.

Breathing Room

I breathe today, automatic, slightly asthmatic,
my voice squeezes out breath, water vapor. Breath,
holding us alive, is slightly blue. Water molecules
absorb red on the color spectrum at atomic speed.

Who teaches color values on the human spectrum?
What color are you when revolving red lights
pull your vehicle over?

Are you so polite your mother would wonder at you,
and is your little stash well secured or didn't you know
your passenger had some, coming into Florida
headed back to school? Did you pull over
for a Texas officer to pass but failed to signal?
Were you pulled over in St. Paul for a fix-it ticket?
Did you head out for an early jog around Fenway Park
in your cold-morning hoodie, a knife in your sock,
keys between your fingers? Were you out for a drive
with friends? For a walk to buy some milk?

What color are you? Will your breath, weaponized,
choke out of you for a mistake or no reason?

Unlike breath, the sky is every rainbow color,
assembled yet scattered molecules, blue most of all.

Call it breathing room, concept we relearn to live
together these plague days, even as skies radiate light,
even as someone's breath is stoppered on a highway
or familiar neighborhood.

And red? Lightwaves of red are longest, take longer
to reach us. Blood-red, passion-red, chances at life
finite in any ordinary month.
And blue—like a trace of shadow—
pulsing code red to reconnect.

Night Crossing

They cross the Rio Grande
from Piedras Negras to Eagle Pass.

River shunts grit, sands legs
scraping black stone bottom.

Night water laps hunger. No time
for the shallow season.

Clutch another's hand and another
rising like weather-beaten prayers,

and fall on side-shoving currents.
Lift each other past hell-drops

between boulders.

Searchlights scan sand islands
where migrant birds scrape beds

lined in bits of shell, pebble, stone.
Speckled life holds for a week—

yet all may wash below.
Silence floods across.

Or from Sabratha on the Libyan coast
past Malta to Sicily and north,

skiffs rock on overload.
Voiceless babes in salt air

clot beaches boats could not land.

Gleaning

Food bank lineup,
neighborly encounters.
I drop off pancake mix,
cold sausage, chocolate
milk—our fundraiser
cancelled in Covid-time.

Homeless men and women
on downtown streets so long
pantry workers greet them
as friends in odd vicinity
not entirely strangers,
not completely known.

Housed locals enter quietly
depart quickly
or accept offers of
door-step delivered meals.

A woman not far
mails surgical masks
to her roofless brother
by way of a man knowing
his creekside camp.

Is a mendicant holding a bowl
on pilgrimage less hungry
than a homeless soul
with family keeping distance?

Finger-ping of the bowl is a bell,
attention to the virtue of less.
Roofless man is attended
by his own practical credo.

In Paris rushing up a Metro stairway,
I passed a child,
hand cupped to the crowd,
woman leaned beside her,
eyes to the floor.

Wrong train, running down
deserted steps in time
to catch the woman
scold the empty girl.

Picking these words
for thought, not work,
leaves me wanting
meals to give
instead of memory.

Cured

Jackrabbit bolted up the drive. Comically
tall ears up and frozen like his heart
behind chamise. Statue hiding.

Our car-monster rumbled by
bringing roofless Mike to dinner,
homemade. Tugged his cap low,

eyes like the hare running,
nowhere real to hide. Wary
glances, beard barbed

quills ready to embed
curious anyones muzzling too close.
His visor cave

shields his shadow eyes from ours
strobing, attentive to his hope.
Will open a bank account

with a first Social check.
Will call mom with the news.
She, a weathered rock inert

in her chair, in the home closed
to his breakage—mason's body,
dry-outs, edges.

And dad, days eighty-proof
yet functions. Public accolades.
Chilled family blood flows

to Mike's thin bedroll.
What chemical brew
composes any of them

or me? Indicates a path? Chance
finding Mike salvaged:
tobacco butt unused

as if pouched with new leaf,
not yet combusted.

Nothing Obvious

He's bedding down, Mike is, in the P.O. lobby,
old sleeping bag, backpack at his head.

Sleeps in an open spot so no one'll think
he's lurking in the dark. Leaves in the a.m.
when workers arrive, sits days nearby,
sketches or shuffles to the food bank.

Beard, wisp of flame going gray
like his dad in a photo,
accepting alumni honors
from his Ivy alma mater.

Clothing, close to clean
from the local laundromat,
where houseless people go, as we did once,
waiting on a washer-dryer delivery.

Mike's lobby spot holds old building jobs,
ten thousand dollars lost in a bad land deal,
ex-wife's number, native plants and flowers
he names near the family home he's barred from
—all packed in a flannel shirt, jeans, work boots.

One day he quietly told two anti-gay bashers
they were wrong—no drama, nothing
to draw attention. He holds a place among us,
who discreetly check ATM deposits, heating bills,
holiday cards, and fold some tender in his hand.

**After nine years on the streets, Mike (a pseudonym) moved into a government "Section 8" studio apartment in a city near his family home and receives Medicaid in-home care.*

After The Diagnosis

Pop keeps hands busy across the page
as synapses try to swing messages
across gaps like trapeze artists
who land through the big top
of his cranium, where he thinks he is
waiting for the show, but numb nerve tips
reach shrinking platforms. Greatest
of ease grows labored, quicksilver
thinking drops tangled in sawdust,
audience works hard to see in silence.

In the closet space between his shirts
hanging undone after the diagnosis,
cuffs brush front to back, touch
of reassurance in the motionless dark.
Split logs stacked in the living room
rest on each other, await release
into the wood stove, gentle
kindling placement in the black box,
transmuted to flame, they are, and ash,
service of pine beyond its green time.

Blue Tattoo

Remains of quail dust baths
dimple the dawn driveway.
Bellies to gravel, wingtips out.
Grit & powder storm.

Nearby a crushed crescent
of carbon blue, maroon.
Artery & vein in one. Nightcrawler,
if only you'd slipped your skin,
twirled inside a spare,
breaststroked away.

Drill & engineer no longer
whirling tunnels through darkness,
the undecorated work,
burrowing earth space
for root-sprawl
in our growing grounds.

I know I'm wishing facts too late
to move your unarmed body
off this metal battlefield.
You may as well swim
on stars now.

Milk moon frays in a blue tattoo.
Sun arrives leaf by leaf,
aligns their spines,
nuzzles pores.
Shadows retreat
beneath stones.

Grief Travel

Grief is love that has nowhere to go,
someone said. But grief gets busy
winding love through every hollow
of our empty, rattling bodies.
Echoes when you wash, dress,
fill with a lost voice,
enter your heart,
boulder of lockdown.
Grief twines love around our ankles,
makes us stumble,
seals our mouths for a time.
Mother grief that drops us
to our knees.
Fathers of grief
who lost their powers
before they fell.
Child grief that learns
to stop asking why.
Grief-travel strips bones
as it slumps green over grey
destiny.
Grief has many ways
to shepherd our love
before it's done,
before it reopens doors,
lets love set off, finding
a new direction, new compass.

Aubade: Farewell And Hello

Morning, a feather
my weightless eyes
followed to the ceiling.
Bedroom quiet,
my fingertips tapped your mouth,
eyes drawn to blue-grey
oceans I slipped into,
not sure what I was,
fragment
shell
bone
of your body.
Words skimmed windows
clouds steered past.

Was I already leaving?
Restless bird
solemn at eclipses
—moon checks sun
waiting on twilight.

Leaving the backyard stream
hemmed in chainlink,
humor well-loved,
well-used, used up.
Thoughts ironed crisp
for the world,
muted prayers
like crabapples
flowering trees
outside the kitchen.

Leaving for red rock canyons,
sage, coyote brush.
Red fox, rust flanks
color of Colorado.

Heart built on shadows
dispelled by Flatirons.
Cirrus mornings
dry-brushed tendrils,

jazz notes curled long,
high. Star-splattered sky
synchronized my breath.

Bird Watching

High-stepping New Mexico Northern Jacana
totes his chick underwing to good insect sites.
Mom rarely goes, so well partnered
to her big pinion, big foot mate.

A randy lass, tho', with multiple Jacs,
an egg-a-nest. Preserve the stock,
drop the eggs, let the fellas take over.
They keep 'em out of rain, warm in shade.

In a day or two, easy peasy: bug field trip.
Dad's egg-yellow forehead leads,
outshines even his lime underwing.
(How the gals noticed when he batched it!)

Oh, to be snuggled beneath that comfy blanket,
safe in dad's arm,
held tight for the trip to school.

Scraggly fluffhead pops up, looks back
over big shoulders toward home.
And mom will be mom will be...

Well, in a month they fledge
for their own bugs.
Unused to flying, though,
some often stray into Texas—

TGIF, Day Off

We stand at attention
before the gate, waiting for it to open.
Or someone to walk up the hill and unlatch it
—the lady who released us from her corral.

Or something,
so we can amble into back acres
wander up the mesa
down the back slope
away from buildings, fences,
visitors wanting rides
on saddles they slip around,
pulling reins, not pressing a knee.

Black white cream roan chestnut.
We herd together in patient time,
lower our necks
muscled and beautiful.

If pure energy of relaxed athletes
could open the gate, we might.
Even though we consider leaping over,
we wait—polite, we like to think—
occasionally reaching
for some ryegrass
or yesterday's alfalfa
but stay turned in the direction
we hope to go,
pretty sure we will.

Except Curt, who from the start
stood back of the crowd
watching the stable.
There's always one
who needs to be
first to know.
This too, we rely on.

Between Tides

Winter shoulder, cusp of spring,
pearly yarrow hour
before bud-break,
before iris sepals
fall in tongues
of startling symmetry.
Soft dreams slip through
pores in the land
ready to store long nights,
raise rows of morning.
Leave complications of approval,
hike to the old meadow
—vanished hunting ground
surrendered to pine-fringed rills.
Chickadees chitter,
horned owls sleep in green towers,
red-tailed hawks sweep through
doug fir, buckeye
above deer beds.

Light showers stipple the bay.
We canoe in shallows
close as falcons fly
to the once-haunted interior,
slide beneath a willow canopy.
Late winter leaves linger,
sluice rivulets of rain
to companion blades
—bright cascade,
sailing cave not bereft.

Between tides breathing
to the moon's slow pull,
our hands on oars
rest like sparrows.

How May We Be

In the open space at land's end
surf sky mix, elixir of sighs.
Wild grasses brush my only body;
I set loose their seed.
The poppies bow; I nod back.
Burrowing worms, apostles of soil,
unpack earth from their pockets.
I trace their roof everywhere,
taste salt in the light of the sea,
honey from bees
on bread I break
with gulls assembled
at the coast oak, vestments ruffling
in the eye of our tabernacle,
my method of prayer,
delight and one life. Yet
out of the flux and flow
silver glint and blue
where we began, how we return
home becomes a salmon scent,
desire a magnet pushing muscle
rising engorged incarnadine
rough bed tossed, gifts laid to gravel
lotus earth on edge turning
en pointe rising—
rise up in league with oceans
push with your mighty lives.

Never Say Never

In Spring, constant swirl,
barn swallows in new days,
lapis blue and ginger.
A thousand swoops to the bay
for grass and mud dabs.

Nest cups an eave
above the back door
unless misty nights
slide it down, unknotted
nuggets on wet grass.

Weightless as air,
they rebuild.
Nothing given or assumed.
Not strong as steel.
Busy artisans.

Survival Skills

A coast redwood tree will sprout new trees from its roots [... in a circle]. The trees grow tall and strong together as they are cared for by the parent tree's roots. Sempervirens Fund

Spring, a green blade.
A man shears sapling redwood
en masse in the morning,

family close to his cabin
framed of harvested forebears.
Sharp cuts to young bodies,

perfect, prime, soft
inverted Vs vertically stacked,
two-inch rocket assemblies

ready for launch,
until he scuttles a thousand missions.
Mothership's roots re-stabilize

who remains, send familiar madre
message: *eat your veggies.*
She recovers steady as time,

sooner than forever, autumn shoots
slip through humus to evening fog,
rise around her.

Quiet beyond his hearing,
pared down to the last safe atom
of night, they lift away.

Generations

...make your decisions on behalf of the seven generations coming,
so that they may enjoy what you have today.
Oren Lyons (Seneca), Faithkeeper, Onondaga Nation

still, moonrise occurs
as expected, still moonrise
cool elliptic disc spirals light
around the globe
'til night hours drain still.

sun climbs by degrees, silver
pink-saffron blazes cerulean,
surrounds swallows in & out
mud-dab nest below the eave,
whip through air for breakfast.

from pines & madrone
swells of fogdrip slow to still.
deer step in through fencetrim
prim down hill, noses up,
tail-twitching time.

still, less is more, more is less,
more of us, more & more
parts per million rise, still.

up the road farmer Albert
won't let land go baked & still.
son of survivors
who brought their dairy skills,
he gathers bovine burps
& hind release, methane
capture closes power loop.

still, be less of more-&-more,
power down
subdue ourselves
ambering specks of life
slower than birds
still lower than ridges,
unable to leap tall buildings.

be nature's own,
thank you, a choice
flora fauna living,
still generations on.

What The Grass Said About Your Return

They crowd in rough,
the memories,
attempted replacements
after you set out,
quiet wandering
through uncut night
curled under leaves
done tacking toward the sun,
exhale in the dark
sweet as rain on creek stones.

Thin clouds cross the moon
between branches
outside my window.
Minute by minute
the yellow circle
draws higher,
smaller,
though I never see it move.
White light surrounds limbs
'til that's gone too.

Grass in its tongues whispers
of greening joy
beneath silver roses. You return
with morning gleam of filament
threaded from brambles
to metal hinging the kitchen door.
Jays scrabble on screeching deck rails,
finches claim their mīnute dignities.

Ghostlight

Lying under the stars,/in the summer night.
Rexroth, The Heart of Heracles

Sheet lightning everywhere & gone
flips day from night,
flares tree specters, rim of earth
outlined in afterglow.

Lightning cracks javelins
across a lake, sizzles sweet willow
or swamp weed to ash.

A man, maybe a thousand years ago,
startled, toppled from a cliff
dwelling high above feral danger
as a woman still-birthed.

Science, cause & effect,
solved ancient mysteries of thunder,
where the sun goes,
changes of season.

Yet here I am under the sky,
this raised cat's hair summer night,
tracing flickers of blazes like gods
beaming two dippers and the North Star.

The Real Mirage

Flying white petals swirl
a cyclone of light
across the four-way.
Riveted to our seats,
drivers pause at the real mirage,
windshields arched in pollen dust.

The giant flower knit by air and angle
whisks through
the wind-whipped crossing
to a narrow street
curbed in stenciled numbers,
broken sidewalks.

Landscape edging catches it
to settle down at houses
swathed in wires, antennae
searching for gamer downloads,
news or music mixes,

while these silent slices
of summer DNA
signal bare feet, sunflowers
big as baseball mitts,
runners sliding into second.

One hot child's day,
I hosted a puppet show,
playmates below my window.
Tiger, teddy, bunny
entered the *commedia* frame.
My buds, magicians
in cahoots with enchantment,
screeched story bits.

Long out of fairy tales, I know
they were preface
to the apparition here and gone,
spun on blacktop guiding me
from this page to arrival.

Incarnata

Autumn walks back time. Short days
return light to the sun heading south.
Wild rose offers her hips,
toyon oak holds out berries
to shrub and garden birds
staying close to home.

We nurture purple aster, blanket flower,
hope monarch butterflies sip nectar
in warm California gardens.
Their endangered hearts beat
for milkweed, shy thistle pretender
who bleeds white pitch, bears thorns
softer than a blush rose.

Monarch larvae lace to this plant only,
formally named Incarnata, life spirit.
We were asked to plant it to help them
and did. On long nights we dream
roots reach deep springs.

Reclamation

Rare snowflakes pile
like end of days,
quiet vehicle columns
cross the bridge.
Late afternoon
lime and ginger time
siphons dry air
astringent. Breath pixels
add up to pale peach,
all the sky accepts
on a fall day.

Shut navy base,
shattered concrete
reaps pummels of battles it taught.
Stream flow it drowned
once gifted the bay,
slipped fog on serpentine,
fed willow, pickle weed,
coast live oak's
forgiving canopy.

Unburied piece of Pacific coast
borrowed
from what we forgot,
moves the pendulum back
a notch in time
linked with sea churn,
moon's silent hand
unclaimed.

What's To Come

I cup the back of her small head
—globe contains worlds,
ponders blue view,
matches chirrups & trills to source.

Sparkle of shiny objects shapes her.
No patinated skin, not yet.
Touches her palms to the rug,
varnished chair leg, velour pillow
smooth, then bristles.

She kicks & shuffles through
leaf-scatter & crackle.
Gust in the oak tells it,
let go leathered ones,
copper, red, burgundy fringe.

She studies their veins,
graph lines scratched in
from midrib
to each prickled point.

Acorns in watch caps await rain
to soak next year's sprig:
seedlings she finds
almost lost in shadow,
ready to spring out.

Rare Glow

Daughter, you'll stare often into mirrors
your long life. Now waves of your hair

drape you in shadow as you curl like a babe
shielding yourself. Sweetheart,

lift your head. You douse other light.
Your flame so new, mulling the world

and your place. Let me praise your first success,
becoming XX, a force apart from XY.

Crossings, junctions always you, exquisite
like rhodium, singular element

lining precious mirrors, more desired
than gold or diamonds,

pings light to faultless gazes like yours.
For umpteen reasons joy

is heliotrope's vanilla scent
or watermelon dissolving in your mouth.

But you don't need to explain. We know
it's dark behind us. We feel it

coating the backs of our eyes. Yet honey,
you are bioluminescence.

Flynn

Flynn rap-dances all day long
on Main Street, flying black beard,
backwards ballcap, T-shirt vest.
Visitors stare at 10-mile speed.
We don't complain, give a wave.

Flynn came back home
a puzzle to us.
Freewheels lyrics conjured
from news, mystics, sources
he knows, lays rhyme inside.

On a bench a homeless man
feels the music flow
through Flynn's arms
& twirling legs, raising
a jubilee of joy.

The man's shoulders jump
to a beat, maybe in time,
maybe his own,
maybe a tune
he and Flynn have heard.

Riddle or lesson, Flynn
exposes us
to cerebration,
cogitation
answering his spirit.

Dance away, break away,
pirouette, Flynn,
to your ecstatic,
telegraphic,
virtuosic song
on footloose terms
you arrived with,
treat us with,
make us jive with
in this maybe offbeat,
maybe safe old town.

I Zoomed Into The Reading

Crowd listened in Zoom boxes
to a rounded poem, illusory
life moments, supernal language.

But I began to feel we were on a bus,
strangers on wobbly wheels,
suppressed throat-clearing, unmuted,
a man in his pajama top, a woman
leaning off-screen signaling a pup
or picking up lint.

I pictured the necklace of ancient snails
you gave me: night dwellers
toting spiral homes on their backs.

Understory lives still inch
dark passages beneath our feet
or surface in daylight on walls, stones,
like keys to lost survival skills,
spells we wander above,
almost severed from earth language.

Alive in my dark dresser drawer,
the necklace sent me home to you
and evening bullfrogs across the field
calling females to amplex froggy-style
in pond shallows. Quick silence
as they slipped beneath leaves or mud.

In the kitchen, roasting potatoes—purple,
red, gold—baked-in specks of loamy soil
we grew them in, pulled them gently out of.

It's Not Your Song That Needs To Rhyme

The stars must knock themselves out,
cacophony of bursting gases, fire.
Heat swirls nowhere we know
on Earth.

Our own star speeds end of days
I'd like to stop from setting.
But we'd lose sparrow song
pull morning from the sky.

I don't need speed of comets
to make my universe sing,
just finches arranging personal space,
wiping beaks back & forth
across branches
after a stop at the water bowl.

When the cat carried in a goldfinch,
yellow chest pounding
soundless behind a dresser,
you lowered your palm
—manacle, it must have seemed—
around his soft fright.

Released out the front door
he shot away, shouting his song.

Now night stretches across your face.
Minutes ago, pressure check
crinkled cuff puffed on your arm,
glance at a screen.
Number over number, fraction
willing your heartbeats to rhyme.

You're Invited

Come & join us, old friend,
for sociable masked mingling
on our sunny deck.

We'll sprinkle gold dust
between ghost hugs
—or at least, golden wild oats
hand-milled in the kitchen,
our own *kintsugi* mending time apart.

Anna's hummer will zip in
for a deep chat with lemon blossoms,
zig out by way of pink geraniums.

We'll sangria-toast evergreens
tracing ridge lines,
as we fit inside these moments
like spruce needles growing
one by one around the same branch.

Stories may tumble out,
how we wriggled & squiggled
on the ground as kids. No worries
come darkly will divide us
or stop jeweled foam curling on the bay.

We'll ask how earthworms manage
five hearts—looking after touch,
taste, hearing, smell
& detecting tonic darkness—
when holding our one intact
is a daily grace & mystery.

This will be our practice,
to celebrate reconnecting
& impermanence
of present maladies,
bless each other's company,
as invisible receptors
around & in us shift
from afternoon to evening
& see-you-very-soons.

Lynn Axelrod has an undergraduate degree in Literature and taught freshman Lit. and Comp. while in a graduate English program. She published her first poetry book at ten years old, typing and binding a set of poems with ribbon for her mother's birthday.

She grew up around artists, their daily studio time, discussions about shows, galleries, museums, tools, materials, news. In her teens she sculpted in clay, an immersive, meditative time.

Post-grad school, Lynn became a lawyer in property and land use. After a decade, she rebalanced her life with more gratifying work: environmental NGO staffer, weekly newspaper reporter, studio jewelry maker, fundraiser for an undergraduate diversity program, and disaster readiness/community organizer for her local fire department.

She returned to her roots in poetry via a long-running group and workshops. Lynn likes to study history—modern, ancient, and in the arts. She volunteers politically and, with her husband, lives in an arts & activist community along the Northern California coast.

www.ingramcontent.com/pod-product-compliance
Lightning Source LLC
LaVergne TN
LVHW090539110826
845146LV00003B/1185

* 9 7 9 8 8 8 8 3 8 5 6 3 0 *